tapas & Spanish food

THE AUSTRALIAN Women's Weekly

contents

tapas 4

lunch 34

dinner 52

dessert 66

glossary 74

conversion chart 77

index 78

Cooking your own Spanish feast is easy, not to mention the perfect way to entertain. Spanish cuisine has a wonderful variety of delicious flavours, and most recipes are created for sharing among friends and family. Choose some of these fantastic recipes to prepare for a day of great company and fabulous food.

Pamela Clark

Editorial & Food Director

Australian cup and spoon measurements are metric. A conversion chart appears on page 77.

tapas

These delicious little mouthfuls are enjoyed in the early evening with a glass of sangria or sherry, and are the most loved of all Spanish food. Try some tonight.

white sangria

- **2 large green apples (400g), unpeeled, sliced thinly**
- **½ cup (125ml) lime juice**
- **1.5 litres (6 cups) riesling**
- **½ cup (125ml) white rum**
- **⅓ cup (80ml) apple schnapps**
- **½ cup (80g) pure icing (confectioners') sugar**
- **3 cups (525g) seedless green grapes, halved**
- **2 cups (300g) fresh blueberries**
- **3 cups (750ml) sparkling mineral water**
- **ice cubes, for serving**

1 Place apple in a medium bowl with juice; stand 5 minutes.

2 Place undrained apples in a large jug with remaining ingredients; stir to combine. Cover; refrigerate 3 hours or overnight.

3 Add ice to the jug just before serving.

makes 3 litres (12 cups)
nutritional count per 1 cup (250ml) 0.1g total fat (0g saturated fat); 869kJ (208 cal); 22.4g carbohydrate; 0.8g protein; 1.4g fibre

tip Only fresh blueberries can be used in this recipe, as frozen berries will tint the sangria.

PREP & COOK TIME
1 HOUR 30 MINS
(+ REFRIGERATION)

tip Salted cod, also known as salt cod, *baccalà*, *bacalhau*, *bacalao* and *morue*, is available from Italian, Spanish and Portuguese delicatessens and some speciality food stores. It needs to be de-salted and rehydrated before use.

cod and olive fritters

- **650g (1¼ pounds) salted cod fillet, skin on**
- **3 medium potatoes (600g), halved**
- **1 tablespoon olive oil**
- **1 medium brown onion (150g), chopped finely**
- **2 cloves garlic, crushed**
- **¼ cup finely chopped fresh flat-leaf parsley**
- **½ cup (60g) seeded green olives, chopped finely**
- **1 egg**
- **vegetable oil, for deep-frying**

makes 40
nutritional count per fritter 2.6g total fat (0.4g saturated fat); 196kJ (47 cal); 47.4g carbohydrate; 3.6g protein; 0.3g fibre

1 Rinse fish under cold water to remove excess salt. Place fish in a large bowl, cover with cold water; refrigerate, covered, overnight, changing the water three or four times. Drain fish; discard water.

2 Place fish in a large saucepan, cover with cold water; bring to the boil, uncovered. Reduce heat; simmer, covered, 5 minutes. Drain fish, discard water; remove skin and bones then flake fish with a fork.

3 Boil, steam or microwave potato until tender; drain. Roughly mash in a large bowl.

4 Meanwhile, heat olive oil in a large frying pan; cook onion and garlic, stirring, until onion softens.

5 Combine fish, onion mixture, parsley, olives and egg with potato.

6 Roll level tablespoons of the mixture into balls, place on a baking paper-lined tray; refrigerate 30 minutes.

7 Heat vegetable oil in a deep medium saucepan; deep-fry fritters, in batches, until browned and heated through. Drain on absorbent paper.

lemon chilli chicken and chorizo skewers

- **400g (12½ ounces) chicken breast fillets, cut into 2cm (¾-inch) pieces**
- **2 cured chorizo sausages (340g), cut into 2cm (¾-inch) pieces**
- **1 medium yellow capsicum (bell pepper) (200g), cut into 2cm (¾-inch) pieces**
- **12 fresh bay leaves**
- **1 tablespoon finely grated lemon rind**
- **1 tablespoon lemon juice**
- **¼ cup (60ml) olive oil**
- **2 cloves garlic, crushed**
- **1 teaspoon dried chilli flakes**
- **¼ cup finely chopped fresh flat-leaf parsley**

1 Combine ingredients in a large bowl; season. Cover; refrigerate 30 minutes.

2 Thread chicken, chorizo, capsicum and bay leaves, alternately, onto 12 skewers.

3 Cook skewers on a heated oiled grill plate (or grill or barbecue) until chicken is cooked through and chorizo is browned lightly.

tips Soak 12 bamboo skewers in boiling water for 10 minutes before using, to prevent them from scorching during cooking. If fresh bay leaves are unavailable, use dried ones and soak them with the skewers. Use any coloured capsicum you like.

makes 12
nutritional count
per skewer 15.3g total fat (4.4g saturated fat); 832kJ (199 cal); 1.3g carbohydrate; 14.3g protein; 0.4g fibre

PREP & COOK TIME
45
MINUTES

roasted thyme potatoes with spicy sauce

- 500g (1 pound) baby new potatoes, halved
- 2 tablespoons olive oil
- 1 tablespoon finely chopped fresh thyme

spicy sauce

- 1 tablespoon olive oil
- 1 small brown onion (80g), chopped finely
- 2 cloves garlic, sliced thinly
- 1 fresh small red thai (serrano) chilli, chopped finely
- 400g (12½ ounces) canned crushed tomatoes
- 2 teaspoons caster (superfine) sugar

1 Preheat oven to 220°C/425°F.

2 Combine potatoes, oil and thyme in a large baking dish; roast about 30 minutes or until potato is tender.

3 Meanwhile, make spicy sauce.

4 Serve spicy sauce with hot roasted potatoes.

spicy sauce Heat oil in a medium saucepan; cook onion, garlic and chilli, stirring, until onion softens. Add undrained tomatoes and sugar; bring to the boil. Reduce heat; simmer, uncovered, stirring occasionally, about 10 minutes or until sauce thickens.

serves 8
nutritional count per serving 7g total fat (1g saturated fat); 506kJ (121 cal); 11.5g carbohydrate; 2.1g protein; 2.2g fibre

PREP & COOK TIME
40
MINUTES

chorizo and potato fritters

- 2 teaspoons vegetable oil
- 1 cured chorizo sausage (170g), chopped finely
- 1 small brown onion (80g), chopped finely
- 2 fresh small red thai (serrano) chillies, chopped finely
- 2 medium zucchini (240g), grated coarsely
- 450g (14½ ounces) bintje potatoes, grated coarsely
- 1 small kumara (orange sweet potato) (250g), grated coarsely
- 3 eggs, beaten lightly
- 1 cup (150g) plain (all-purpose) flour
- 1 teaspoon sweet paprika
- vegetable oil, for deep-frying

sweet chilli dipping sauce

- ½ cup (120g) sour cream
- 2 tablespoons sweet chilli sauce

1 Heat vegetable oil in a medium frying pan; cook chorizo, onion and chilli, stirring, until onion softens. Add zucchini; cook, stirring, 1 minute. Cool 10 minutes.

2 Meanwhile, make sweet chilli dipping sauce.

3 Combine chorizo mixture in a large bowl with potato, kumara, egg, flour and paprika.

4 Heat oil in a large saucepan; deep-fry level tablespoons of mixture, in batches, until fritters are browned lightly. Drain on absorbent paper. Serve fritters with sweet chilli dipping sauce.

sweet chilli dipping sauce Combine sour cream and sauce in a small bowl.

makes 40
nutritional count per fritter 4.6g total fat (1.1g saturated fat); 309kJ (74 cal); 5.3g carbohydrate; 2.6g protein; 0.6g fibre

- 180g (5½ ounces) light cream cheese, softened
- 2 tablespoons lemon juice
- a few drops Tabasco sauce
- 110g (3½ ounces) canned sardines in spring water, drained, mashed
- 1 shallot (25g), chopped finely
- 2 teaspoons finely chopped fresh flat-leaf parsley
- ¼ teaspoon cracked black pepper

1 Beat cream cheese, juice and sauce in a small bowl with an electric mixer until smooth.

2 Stir in remaining ingredients until combined; season to taste.

serving suggestions Sprinkle with extra finely chopped fresh flat-leaf parsley; serve with crusty bread or crackers.

sardine dip

tip Tabasco is the brand name of an extremely fiery sauce made from vinegar and red thai chillies. Use according to taste.

PREP & COOK TIME 10 MINUTES

makes 1 cup
nutritional count per tablespoon 11.7g total fat (6.6g saturated fat); 652kJ (156 cal); 2.4g carbohydrate; 10.3g protein; 0.2g fibre

serves 8
nutritional count per serving 23.7g total fat (4.8g saturated fat); 1409kJ (337 cal); 6.9g carbohydrate; 23.7g protein; 0.7g fibre

crispy marinated whitebait

- **1kg (2 pounds) fresh or frozen whitebait**
- **½ cup (125ml) red wine vinegar**
- **4 cloves garlic, crushed**
- **2 tablespoons finely chopped fresh oregano**
- **1 fresh small red thai (serrano) chilli, chopped finely**
- **1 teaspoon cracked black pepper**
- **½ cup (75g) plain (all-purpose) flour**
- **vegetable oil, for deep-frying**
- **¼ cup loosely packed fresh oregano leaves**

1 Combine whitebait, vinegar, garlic, chopped oregano, chilli and pepper in a large bowl. Cover; refrigerate 3 hours or overnight.

2 Drain the whitebait, pat dry with absorbent paper.

3 Toss whitebait and flour together in a large bowl; season.

4 Heat vegetable oil in a large saucepan; deep-fry oregano a few seconds or until crisp. Drain on absorbent paper.

5 Deep-fry whitebait, in batches, until browned lightly. Drain on absorbent paper. Serve topped with deep-fried oregano.

fried oysters with salsa

- 1 small tomato (90g), chopped finely
- ½ medium yellow capsicum (bell pepper) (100g), chopped finely
- ½ medium red onion (85g), chopped finely
- 1 tablespoon finely chopped fresh coriander (cilantro)
- 1 tablespoon olive oil
- 1 tablespoon lime juice
- 1 fresh small red thai (serrano) chilli, seeded, chopped finely
- 12 oysters on the half shell
- ½ cup (85g) polenta
- ⅓ cup (80ml) milk
- 1 egg, beaten lightly
- pinch cayenne pepper
- vegetable oil, for deep-frying

1 Preheat oven to 180°C/350°F.
2 Combine tomato, capsicum, onion, coriander, olive oil, juice and chilli in a small bowl; season to taste.
3 Remove oysters from shells; reserve oysters. Place shells on an oven tray; heat in the oven 5 minutes.
4 Meanwhile, combine polenta, milk, egg and pepper in a small bowl.
5 Heat vegetable oil in a medium saucepan. Dip oysters in batter; deep-fry oysters, in batches, until browned lightly. Drain on absorbent paper. Return oysters to shells; top with salsa.

makes 12
nutritional count per oyster 5.5g total fat (1g saturated fat); 276kJ (66 cal); 6.1g carbohydrate; 2.9g protein; 0.5g fibre

PREP & COOK TIME
40
MINUTES

soft shell crabs with green onion aïoli

- ½ cup (100g) rice flour
- 1 teaspoon dried chilli flakes
- 2 teaspoons sea salt flakes
- 8 uncooked small soft shell crabs (500g)
- vegetable oil, for deep-frying
- 1 cup loosely packed fresh basil leaves

green onion aïoli

- ¾ cup (225g) mayonnaise
- 2 green onions (scallions), sliced thinly
- 1 clove garlic, crushed
- 1 tablespoon lemon juice

1 Make green onion aïoli.
2 Combine flour, chilli and salt in a medium bowl.
3 Clean crabs; pat dry then cut into quarters. Coat crabs with flour mixture; shake off excess.
4 Heat oil in a large saucepan; deep-fry basil about 30 seconds or until crisp. Drain on absorbent paper. Deep-fry crabs, in batches, until browned lightly. Drain on absorbent paper.
5 Serve crabs with basil, aïoli and lemon wedges, if you like.

green onion aïoli Combine ingredients in a small bowl.

tip To clean the soft shell crabs, lift back the flap on undersides and wipe clean with a damp piece of absorbent paper. Never wash soft shell crab under a running tap as this will wash away the "sea" flavour. If you need to rinse, hold it over the sink and gently splash it with a little water.

serves 8
nutritional count per serving 13g total fat (1.5g saturated fat); 920kJ (220 cal); 16.7g carbohydrate; 9g protein; 0.6g fibre

orange-glazed squid

- 750g (1½ pounds) small squid hoods
- 3 cloves garlic, crushed
- 1 teaspoon sweet paprika
- 2 teaspoons finely grated orange rind
- 1 tablespoon orange juice
- 1 tablespoon red wine vinegar
- ¼ cup (55g) firmly packed light brown sugar
- 1 tablespoon olive oil
- 1 tablespoon finely chopped fresh coriander (cilantro)

1 Cut squid down centre to open out; cut into 5cm (2-inch) pieces.

2 Combine squid, garlic, paprika, rind, juice, vinegar, sugar and oil in a medium bowl. Cover; refrigerate 3 hours or overnight.

3 Drain squid; reserve marinade. Cook squid in a heated oiled large frying pan, in batches, until browned lightly and tender. Remove from pan.

4 Add reserved marinade to the pan; bring to the boil. Reduce heat; simmer, uncovered, about 1 minute or until thickened slightly.

5 Combine squid and marinade mixture with coriander in a large bowl; season to taste.

serves 8
nutritional count per serving 3.4g total fat (0.7g saturated fat); 510kJ (122 cal); 7g carbohydrate; 15.8g protein; 0.2g fibre

PREP & COOK TIME
30
MINUTES
(+ REFRIGERATION)

eggplant fritters

- **2 large eggplants (1kg)**
- **1 cup (100g) coarsely grated mozzarella cheese**
- **½ cup coarsely chopped fresh flat-leaf parsley**
- **2 cloves garlic, crushed**
- **½ cup (50g) packaged breadcrumbs**
- **¼ cup (35g) plain (all-purpose) flour**
- **2 eggs**
- **vegetable oil, for shallow-frying**

makes 36
nutritional count per fritter 5.3g total fat (1g saturated fat); 272kJ (65 cal); 2.4g carbohydrate; 1.7g protein; 0.8g fibre

1 Preheat oven to 220°C/425°F.
2 Remove and discard stem ends from eggplants; prick eggplants all over with a fork. Place on an oiled oven tray; roast about 30 minutes or until soft. Cool. Peel eggplants; chop flesh finely.
3 Combine eggplant, cheese, parsley, garlic, breadcrumbs, flour and eggs in a large bowl; season. Using wet hands, shape level tablespoons of the mixture into oval patties.
4 Heat oil in a large frying pan; shallow-fry fritters, in batches, until browned on both sides. Drain on absorbent paper. Serve warm or cold.

PREP & COOK TIME
1
HOUR
(+ COOLING)

PREP & COOK TIME
40
MINUTES

tip Meatballs and sauce can be made a day ahead. To reheat the meatballs, place them in a single layer, on an oven tray; cover with foil, making several slashes in the foil to allow steam to escape. Bake in an oven preheated to 180°C/350°F for about 20 minutes.

spiced meatballs with romesco sauce

- 250g (8 ounces) cured chorizo sausages, chopped coarsely
- 1 small red onion (100g), chopped coarsely
- 2 cloves garlic, crushed
- 500g (1 pound) lean minced (ground) beef
- ½ teaspoon ground nutmeg
- 1 tablespoon dry sherry
- ½ cup (35g) stale breadcrumbs
- olive oil, for shallow-frying

romesco sauce

- 1 teaspoon dried chilli flakes
- 2 cloves garlic, crushed
- 1 tablespoon slivered almonds, roasted
- 2 medium tomatoes (300g), chopped coarsely
- ¼ cup (60ml) extra virgin olive oil
- 1 tablespoon red wine vinegar

1 Make romesco sauce.
2 Blend or process chorizo, onion and garlic, pulsing until ingredients are finely chopped and combined. Transfer mixture to a large bowl; stir in beef, nutmeg, sherry and breadcrumbs; season. Roll level tablespoons of the mixture into balls.
3 Heat oil in a large frying pan; shallow-fry meatballs, in batches, until browned and cooked through. Drain on absorbent paper.
4 Serve meatballs with romesco sauce.

romesco sauce Soak chilli flakes in hot water for 5 minutes; drain. Blend or process chilli, garlic, nuts and tomato until smooth. With motor operating, gradually add combined oil and vinegar in a thin steady stream until sauce is smooth.

makes 40
nutritional count per meatball with sauce
6.7g total fat
(1.6g saturated fat);
343kJ (82 cal);
1.1g carbohydrate;
4.1g protein; 0.3g fibre

- **4 cured chorizo sausages (680g)**
- **1 tablespoon olive oil**
- **2 cloves garlic, crushed**
- **¼ cup finely chopped fresh flat-leaf parsley**

1 Cut chorizo into 5mm (¼-inch) slices.
2 Heat oil in large frying pan; cook chorizo, stirring, until crisp. Add garlic; cook, stirring, 30 seconds. Remove from heat; stir in parsley.

fried chorizo with garlic

serves 8
nutritional count per serving 27.8g total fat (9.6g saturated fat); 1350kJ (323 cal); 2.3g carbohydrate; 16.6g protein; 0.6g fibre

serves 8
nutritional count per serving 10.1g total fat (4.1g saturated fat); 606kJ (145 cal); 0.3g carbohydrate; 13g protein; 0.4g fibre

prawns with garlic herb butter

- **1kg (2 pounds) uncooked medium king prawns (shrimp)**
- **2 tablespoons olive oil**
- **6 cloves garlic, crushed**
- **50g (1½ ounces) butter, chopped coarsely**
- **1 tablespoon lemon juice**
- **2 tablespoons finely chopped fresh flat-leaf parsley**

1 Shell and devein prawns, leaving heads and tails intact.

2 Heat oil in a large frying pan; cook garlic, stirring, until soft. Add prawns; cook, turning, until prawns start to change colour and are almost cooked. Add butter and juice; cook, turning, until prawns are cooked through. Stir in parsley.

serving suggestion Bread rolls and lime wedges.

PREP & COOK TIME
50
MINUTES
(+ COOLING & REFRIGERATION)

paella croquettes

- **1 cup (200g) white long-grain rice**
- **2 cups (500ml) chicken stock**
- **1 dried bay leaf**
- **1 teaspoon ground turmeric**
- **2 teaspoons olive oil**
- **1 clove garlic, crushed**
- **1 medium red onion (170g), chopped coarsely**
- **1 cured chorizo sausage (170g), chopped coarsely**
- **100g (3 ounces) smoked chicken, chopped coarsely**
- **1 tablespoon finely chopped fresh flat-leaf parsley**
- **¼ cup (35g) plain (all-purpose) flour**
- **2 eggs, beaten lightly**
- **1 tablespoon milk**
- **1 cup (100g) packaged breadcrumbs**
- **vegetable oil, for deep-frying**

1 Combine rice, stock, bay leaf and turmeric in a medium saucepan; bring to the boil, stirring. Reduce heat; simmer, covered, about 12 minutes or until rice is tender. Remove from heat; stand, covered, 10 minutes. Fluff rice with a fork, discard bay leaf; cool.

2 Meanwhile, heat olive oil in a large frying pan; cook garlic, onion and chorizo, stirring, until onion softens; cool.

3 Blend or process rice, chorizo mixture, chicken and parsley until ingredients come together; season to taste. Using wet hands, shape ¼ cups of rice mixture into croquettes. Toss croquettes in flour; shake off excess. Dip into combined egg and milk, then into breadcrumbs. Place croquettes on a baking paper-lined tray; cover, refrigerate 30 minutes.

4 Heat vegetable oil in a large saucepan; deep-fry croquettes, in batches, until browned lightly.

makes 12
nutritional count per croquette 13.6g total fat (3.1g saturated fat); 1037kJ (248 cal); 22.3g carbohydrate; 9.2g protein; 0.9g fibre

crumbed sardines with roasted tomato sauce

- 24 butterflied sardines (1kg)
- ¼ cup (35g) plain (all-purpose) flour
- 4 eggs, beaten lightly
- 3½ cups (245g) stale breadcrumbs
- ½ cup finely chopped fresh flat-leaf parsley
- ¼ cup finely chopped fresh oregano
- vegetable oil, for deep-frying

roasted tomato sauce

- 6 medium egg (plum) tomatoes (450g), chopped coarsely
- 4 cloves garlic, peeled
- 2 tablespoons red wine vinegar
- 2 tablespoons light brown sugar
- 1 large brown onion (200g), chopped coarsely
- 2 tablespoons olive oil

1 Make roasted tomato sauce.

2 Meanwhile, coat sardines in flour; shake off excess. Dip sardines into egg, then into combined breadcrumbs and herbs.

3 Heat oil in a large saucepan; deep-fry sardines, in batches, until browned and cooked through. Drain on absorbent paper.

4 Serve sardines with roasted tomato sauce.

roasted tomato sauce Preheat oven to 220°C/425°F. Combine ingredients in a large baking dish. Bake about 30 minutes or until onion softens. Blend or process tomato mixture until smooth; season to taste.

serving suggestion Serve with lemon wedges.

serves 6
nutritional count per serving 42.9g total fat (8.7g saturated fat); 3097kJ (741 cal); 38.8g carbohydrate; 48.4g protein; 3.8g fibre

PREP & COOK TIME
50
MINUTES

lunch

In Spain, the most important meal of the day is lunch. Spaniards enjoy a long lunch later in the afternoon. These recipes provide you with the perfect excuse to enjoy your own long lunch.

- 1¼ cups (310ml) olive oil
- ¾ cup (180ml) dry white wine
- 2 tablespoons lemon juice
- 6 cloves garlic, sliced thinly
- 1 fresh long red chilli, chopped finely
- 1kg (2 pounds) uncooked large king prawns (shrimp)
- ⅓ cup coarsely chopped fresh flat-leaf parsley

1 Preheat oven to 220°C/425°F.
2 Stir oil, wine, juice, garlic and chilli in a large flameproof baking dish over low heat 5 minutes or until fragrant. Cool 15 minutes.
3 Meanwhile, shell and devein prawns, leaving tails intact.
4 Add prawns to oil mixture; mix well. Transfer to oven; cook 10 minutes or until prawns change colour. Season to taste.
5 Spoon prawn mixture into shallow bowls; sprinkle with parsley.

garlic prawns

PREP & COOK TIME 45 MINUTES (+ COOLING)

serving suggestion
Serve with crusty bread.

serves 4
nutritional count per serving 71.4g total fat (10.1g saturated fat); 3227kJ (772 cal); 0.9g carbohydrate; 26.2g protein; 1g fibre

serves 8
nutritional count per serving 9.8g total fat (1.3g saturated fat); 614kJ (147 cal); 5.6g carbohydrate; 6.6g protein; 5.1g fibre

cauliflower with garlic, chilli and anchovies

- **2kg (4 pounds) cauliflower, cut into small florets**
- **⅓ cup (80ml) extra virgin olive oil**
- **2 fresh long red chillies, seeded, chopped finely**
- **4 cloves garlic, chopped finely**
- **6 drained anchovy fillets, chopped finely**
- **1 cup coarsely chopped fresh flat-leaf parsley**
- **2 tablespoons lemon juice**
- **1 medium lemon (140g), cut into wedges**

1 Boil, steam or microwave cauliflower until almost tender; drain well.

2 Heat oil in a large deep frying pan; cook chilli, garlic and anchovy, stirring, until fragrant. Add cauliflower; cook, stirring, until hot. Remove from heat; stir in parsley and juice. Season to taste. Serve with lemon wedges.

tip If you don't have a large frying pan, toss the cauliflower with the anchovy mixture in a wok.

PREP & COOK TIME
45
MINUTES

sardines with tomatoes and caper dressing

- 12 whole sardines (540g), cleaned
- 4 medium egg (plum) tomatoes (300g), sliced thickly
- 1 small red onion (100g), sliced thinly

caper dressing

- ⅓ cup (80ml) red wine vinegar
- ¼ cup (60ml) olive oil
- 1 tablespoon drained, rinsed baby capers
- 1 clove garlic, crushed
- 2 tablespoons coarsely chopped fresh flat-leaf parsley

serves 4
nutritional count per serving 16.3g total fat (2.7g saturated fat); 1091kJ (261 cal); 3.2g carbohydrate; 24.2g protein; 1.5g fibre

1 Remove and discard sardine heads. To butterfly sardines, cut through the underside of fish to the tail. Break backbone at tail; peel away backbone. Trim sardines.

2 Cook sardines on a heated oiled grill plate (or grill or barbecue) until browned on both sides and cooked through.

3 Meanwhile, make caper dressing.

4 Serve sardines with tomato and onion; drizzle with dressing.

caper dressing Place ingredients in a screw-top jar; shake well. Season to taste.

serving suggestion
Serve with crusty bread.

serves 4
nutritional count per serving 29.3g total fat (4.2g saturated fat); 1802kJ (431 cal); 9.1g carbohydrate; 25.3g protein; 4.1g fibre

clams with white wine and tomatoes

- 2.5kg (5 pounds) clams
- ½ cup (125ml) dry white wine
- ½ cup (125ml) olive oil
- 1 small red onion (100g), chopped finely
- 2 cloves garlic, crushed
- 2 tablespoons lemon juice
- 2 tablespoons white wine vinegar
- 5 large tomatoes (1.1kg), chopped coarsely
- 4 green onions (scallions), sliced thinly
- 2 tablespoons coarsely chopped fresh coriander (cilantro)

1 Rinse clams under cold water; place in a large bowl of cold salted water, stand 2 hours. Discard water then rinse clams thoroughly; drain.
2 Place clams in a large saucepan with wine. Cover; bring to the boil. Reduce heat; simmer about 5 minutes or until clams open (discard any that do not). Drain clams; discard liquid.
3 Heat one tablespoon of the oil in the same pan; cook red onion and garlic, stirring, until browned lightly. Add combined juice, vinegar and remaining oil; cook, stirring, about 2 minutes or until thickened slightly.
4 Return clams to the pan with tomato, green onion and coriander; toss gently to combine. Season to taste.

PREP & COOK TIME
40
MINUTES
(+ STANDING)

chicken with lentil salad

- **12 chicken tenderloins (900g)**
- **2 teaspoons each ground cumin and ground coriander**
- **1 teaspoon ground turmeric**
- **1½ cups (300g) red lentils**
- **1 clove garlic, crushed**
- **1 fresh small red thai (serrano) chilli, chopped finely**
- **1 lebanese cucumber (130g), seeded, chopped finely**
- **1 medium red capsicum (bell pepper) (200g), chopped finely**
- **¼ cup (60ml) lemon juice**
- **2 teaspoons peanut oil**
- **2 tablespoons coarsely chopped fresh coriander (cilantro)**
- **2 limes, cut into wedges**

1 Combine chicken and spices in a medium bowl.
2 Cook lentils in a large saucepan of boiling water, uncovered, until tender; drain. Rinse under cold water; drain.
3 Place lentils in a large bowl with garlic, chilli, cucumber, capsicum, juice, oil and fresh coriander; toss gently to combine. Season to taste.
4 Cook chicken on a heated oiled grill plate (or grill or barbecue) until cooked through. Cook limes on same grill plate until browned both sides.
5 Serve chicken with lentil salad and lime wedges.

serves 4
nutritional count per serving 9.1g total fat (2g saturated fat); 2157kJ (516 cal); 31.6g carbohydrate; 70.2g protein; 11.7g fibre

PREP & COOK TIME
25
MINUTES

PREP & COOK TIME
40
MINUTES

tip For a more intense flavour, combine cooked quail and mint dressing in a large bowl; cover, refrigerate 3 hours or overnight. Remove from refrigerator about 30 minutes before serving. Stir in tomato.

quail with tomatoes and mint dressing

- 6 quails (1.2kg)
- 1 teaspoon ground cumin
- 3 cloves garlic, crushed
- ¼ cup (60ml) olive oil
- 2 medium tomatoes (300g), seeded, chopped finely

mint dressing

- ½ cup (125ml) olive oil
- ⅓ cup (80ml) white wine vinegar
- 1 tablespoon finely shredded fresh mint

1 Preheat oven to 180°C/350°F.

2 Rinse quails under cold water; pat dry with absorbent paper. Discard necks from quails. Using kitchen scissors, cut along sides of quails' backbones; discard backbones. Halve quails along breastbones. Combine quail, cumin, garlic and 1 tablespoon of the oil in a large bowl.

3 Heat remaining oil in a large frying pan; cook quail, in batches, until browned. Remove from pan.

4 Place quail, skin-side up, in a single layer on an oven tray; cook, in the oven, about 15 minutes or until cooked through.

5 Meanwhile, make mint dressing.

6 Serve quail drizzled with dressing; sprinkle with tomato.

mint dressing Place ingredients in a screw-top jar; shake well. Season to taste.

serves 6
nutritional count per serving 39.1g total fat (6.9g saturated fat); 1789kJ (428 cal); 0.6g carbohydrate; 18.9g protein; 0.5g fibre

shredded beef soup

- 500g (1-pound) piece beef skirt steak
- 2 litres (8 cups) water
- 1 dried bay leaf
- 6 black peppercorns
- 1 large carrot (180g), chopped coarsely
- 1 stick celery (150g), trimmed, chopped coarsely
- 1 tablespoon olive oil
- 1 medium brown onion (150g), sliced thickly
- 1 medium red capsicum (bell pepper) (200g), sliced thickly
- 1 medium green capsicum (bell pepper) (200g), sliced thickly
- 2 cloves garlic, crushed
- 2 fresh long red chillies, chopped finely
- 1 teaspoon ground cumin
- 400g (12½ ounces) canned crushed tomatoes
- ⅓ cup loosely packed fresh oregano leaves
- 1 trimmed corn cob (250g)

1 Tie beef with kitchen string at 2.5cm (1-inch) intervals. Place in a large saucepan with the water, bay leaf, peppercorns, carrot and celery; bring to the boil. Reduce heat; simmer, covered, 1½ hours. Uncover; simmer about 30 minutes or until beef is tender. Cool beef in stock 10 minutes.

2 Transfer beef to a large bowl; using two forks, shred beef coarsely. Strain stock through muslin-lined sieve over another large heatproof bowl; discard solids.

3 Heat oil in the same cleaned pan; cook onion, capsicum, garlic, chilli and cumin, stirring, until vegetables soften. Return beef and stock to pan with undrained tomatoes and ¼ cup of the oregano; bring to the boil. Reduce heat; simmer, uncovered, 10 minutes.

4 Cut corn kernels from cob. Add corn to soup; cook, uncovered, until just tender. Season to taste.

5 Serve soup sprinkled with remaining oregano.

serving suggestion Serve with toasted flour tortillas.

serves 4
nutritional count per serving 9g total fat (2g saturated fat); 1413kJ (338 cal); 25.9g carbohydrate; 34.3g protein; 7.4g fibre

PREP & COOK TIME
2 HOURS 40 MINS
(+ COOLING)

PREP & COOK TIME
20
MINUTES

serves 6
nutritional count per serving 28.9g total fat (8g saturated fat); 1743kJ (417 cal); 25.3g carbohydrate; 11g protein; 6.7g fibre

Valencian salad

- 6 large oranges (1.8kg), peeled, sliced thinly
- 2 medium tomatoes (300g), sliced thickly
- 1 large red onion (300g), sliced thinly
- 100g (3 ounces) manchego cheese, shaved
- ¾ cup (120g) seeded black olives, halved
- 2 large avocados (640g), chopped coarsely
- 1 cup loosely packed fresh mint leaves

orange dressing

- 2 tablespoons olive oil
- 2 tablespoons red wine vinegar
- 2 tablespoons orange juice
- 1 clove garlic, crushed

1 Make orange dressing.
2 Place orange in a large bowl with remaining ingredients and dressing; toss gently to combine. Season to taste.

orange dressing Place ingredients in a screw-top jar; shake well.

tip Manchego cheese is a sharp, firm Spanish cheese; it can be found in most specialty food stores and delicatessens. You can use parmesan cheese instead, if manchego is not available.

PREP & COOK TIME
1 HOUR 15 MINS

tortilla with tomato salsa

- 2 large potatoes (600g), sliced thinly
- 2 medium brown onions (300g), sliced thinly
- 1 medium red capsicum (bell pepper) (200g), chopped coarsely
- 150g (4½ ounces) green beans, trimmed, chopped coarsely
- 8 eggs
- ¼ cup (60ml) skim milk
- ⅓ cup coarsely chopped fresh flat-leaf parsley

tomato salsa

- 1 large tomato (220g), seeded, chopped finely
- 2 lebanese cucumbers (260g), seeded, chopped finely
- 1 small red onion (100g), chopped finely
- 2 long green chillies, chopped finely
- ¼ cup (60ml) lemon juice
- 2 tablespoons finely chopped fresh coriander (cilantro)

1 Heat an oiled 26cm (10½-inch) frying pan; cook potato and onion, stirring, 2 minutes. Reduce heat; cook, covered, stirring occasionally, 15 minutes. Add capsicum and beans; cook, covered, 5 minutes or until potato is tender. Remove from heat.

2 Whisk eggs, milk and parsley in a large jug, season. Pour egg mixture over potato mixture; stir gently.

3 Return pan to low heat; cook, uncovered, 20 minutes. Cover; cook about 10 minutes or until tortilla is set.

4 Meanwhile, make tomato salsa.

5 Serve tortilla topped with salsa.

tomato salsa Combine ingredients in a small bowl.

serves 6
nutritional count per serving 7.4g total fat (2.2g saturated fat); 1672kJ (200 cal); 18.7g carbohydrate; 14.1g protein; 4.5g fibre

dinner

After a large lunch, a lighter dinner is preferred and normally not served until nine or ten o'clock at night. Seafood is a popular choice, and is often mixed with rice to create paella.

salted cod with roasted tomatoes

- 1.5kg (3 pounds) salted cod fillets, skin on
- 6 large tomatoes (1.3kg)
- ½ cup (125ml) olive oil
- 1 medium brown onion (150g), chopped coarsely
- 2 dried ancho chillies
- ¼ cup (60ml) boiling water
- 500g (1 pound) baby new potatoes, halved
- 4 medium brown onions (600g), chopped finely
- 6 cloves garlic, crushed
- 1 teaspoon smoked paprika
- 1 cup (150g) pimiento-stuffed green olives
- ½ cup coarsely chopped fresh parsley

serves 6
nutritional count per serving 3.8g total fat (0.6g saturated fat); 589kJ (141 cal); 3.1g carbohydrate; 22.7g protein; 1.2g fibre

1 Rinse fish under cold water to remove excess salt. Place fish in a large bowl, cover with cold water; refrigerate, covered, overnight, changing the water three or four times. Drain fish; discard water.

2 Preheat oven to 200°C/400°F.

3 Remove cores from tops of tomatoes; cut a small cross in the skin at base of each tomato. Place on an oiled oven tray, drizzle with 1 tablespoon of the oil; roast 15 minutes or until tomatoes begin to soften. When cool enough to handle, peel away skins.

4 Meanwhile, place fish in a large saucepan with coarsely chopped onion, cover with water; bring to the boil. Reduce heat; simmer, uncovered, 15 minutes or until fish is cooked. Drain fish; discard liquid and onion. Remove skin and bones from fish; flake fish into 4cm (1½-inch) pieces.

5 Place chillies in a bowl, cover with the boiling water; stand 10 minutes. Drain; discard liquid. Remove stems, seeds and membranes from chillies; chop chillies. Blend or process tomatoes and chillies until smooth.

6 Boil, steam or microwave potatoes until tender; drain.

7 Heat remaining oil in a large frying pan; cook finely chopped onion and garlic, stirring, until onion is softened and browned lightly. Add paprika; cook, stirring, 1 minute. Add tomato mixture, fish, potatoes, olives and parsley; season to taste, stir gently until heated through.

tip Salted cod, also called salt cod, *baccalà, bacalhau, bacalao* and *morue*, is available from Italian, Spanish and Portuguese delicatessens and some specialty food stores. It needs to be de-salted and rehydrated before use.

serves 4
nutritional count per serving 23.5g total fat (4.4g saturated fat); 1789kJ (428 cal); 7.4g carbohydrate; 46.9g protein; 5.6g fibre
PREP & COOK TIME
55
MINUTES

fish with green sauce and white bean puree

- 1 tablespoon olive oil
- 1 clove garlic, crushed
- 1 medium brown onion (150g), chopped finely
- 1.2kg (2½ pounds) canned white beans, rinsed, drained
- 1 cup (250ml) chicken stock
- ¼ cup (60ml) pouring cream
- 4 x 200g (6½-ounce) white fish fillets, skin-on

green sauce

- ½ cup finely chopped fresh flat-leaf parsley
- ¼ cup each finely chopped fresh mint, dill and chives
- 1 tablespoon wholegrain mustard
- 2 tablespoons lemon juice
- 2 tablespoons rinsed, drained baby capers, chopped finely
- 1 clove garlic, crushed
- ¼ cup (60ml) olive oil

1 Make green sauce.
2 Heat oil in a medium saucepan; cook garlic and onion, stirring, until onion softens. Add beans and stock; bring to the boil. Reduce heat; simmer, uncovered, until liquid has almost evaporated. Stir in cream; blend or process bean mixture until smooth. Season to taste.
3 Meanwhile, cook fish, skin-side down, in a heated oiled large frying pan, turning once, until cooked as desired.
4 Serve fish on white bean puree, topped with green sauce.
green sauce Combine all ingredients in a small bowl.

tips Many varieties of cooked white beans are available canned, among them cannellini (which is what we used), butter and haricot beans; any of these are suitable for this recipe. We used kingfish in this recipe but you can use snapper or any white fish fillets you like.

PREP & COOK TIME
1 HOUR
20 MINS

chicken with chocolate sauce

- **6 x 500g (1-pound) small chickens**
- **⅓ cup (50g) plain (all-purpose) flour**
- **¼ cup (60ml) olive oil**
- **1 medium brown onion (150g), chopped finely**
- **2 cloves garlic, crushed**
- **1 cinnamon stick**
- **¼ teaspoon ground cloves**
- **½ teaspoon ground nutmeg**
- **800g (1½ pounds) canned crushed tomatoes**
- **1 large red capsicum (bell pepper) (350g), sliced thinly**
- **1 cup (250ml) dry white wine**
- **60g (2 ounces) dark eating (semi-sweet) chocolate, chopped finely**
- **⅓ cup coarsely chopped fresh flat-leaf parsley**

1 Rinse chickens under cold water; pat dry with absorbent paper. Using kitchen scissors, cut along the sides of chickens' backbones; discard backbones. Halve chickens along their breastbones then cut each half into two pieces.
2 Coat chicken in flour; shake off excess. Heat oil in a large frying pan; cook chicken, in batches, until browned. Drain on absorbent paper.
3 Cook onion and garlic in the same pan, stirring, until onion softens. Add spices, cook, stirring, until fragrant.
4 Return chicken to pan with undrained tomatoes, capsicum and wine; simmer, covered, 20 minutes. Uncover; simmer about 20 minutes or until chicken is tender and sauce thickens slightly. Add chocolate; cook, stirring, until smooth. Discard cinnamon stick; season to taste. Serve chicken with sauce; sprinkle with parsley.

serving suggestion
Serve with crusty bread, steamed green beans and rice or a green salad.

serves 6
nutritional count per serving 51.9g total fat (15.3g saturated fat); 3294kJ (788 cal); 20.1g carbohydrate; 52.8g protein; 3.3g fibre

braised chicken with chickpeas, lemon & garlic

- 1 tablespoon olive oil
- 2 medium brown onions (300g), sliced thickly
- 2 teaspoons smoked paprika
- 3 cloves garlic, crushed
- 8 chicken thigh cutlets, skin removed (1.6kg)
- 3 cups (750ml) salt-reduced chicken stock
- ¼ cup (60ml) lemon juice
- 2 fresh long red chillies, halved lengthways
- 800g (1½ pounds) canned chickpeas (garbanzo beans), rinsed, drained
- 2 teaspoons dijon mustard
- ½ cup coarsely chopped fresh flat-leaf parsley
- 2 teaspoons finely grated lemon rind

1 Heat oil in a large casserole dish; cook onion, stirring, until softened. Add paprika, garlic and chicken; stir to coat chicken in onion mixture.

2 Add stock, juice, chilli, chickpeas and mustard to the pan; bring to the boil. Reduce heat; simmer, covered, 30 minutes. Uncover; simmer further 30 minutes or until chicken is tender. Season to taste.

3 Serve chicken sprinkled with parsley and rind.

tip If you prefer, substitute 8 chicken legs or 4 chicken marylands for thigh cutlets. Smoked spanish paprika, also known as pimiento, gives this dish its characteristic Spanish flavour.

serves 4
nutritional count per serving 22.4g total fat (5.6g saturated fat); 2378kJ (569 cal); 24.7g carbohydrate; 63.5g protein; 8.4g fibre

tip Calasparra or bomba are the authentic Spanish rices to use for paella, but arborio rice will do just as well.

seafood paella with aioli

- ½ teaspoon saffron threads
- 2 tablespoons boiling water
- ¼ cup (60ml) olive oil
- 1 large brown onion (200g), chopped finely
- 4 cloves garlic, crushed
- 4 medium tomatoes (600g) chopped finely
- 800g (1½ pounds) uncooked medium king prawns (shrimp)
- 1½ teaspoons smoked paprika
- 1 litre (4 cups) water
- 2 cups (400g) white short-grain rice
- 500g (1 pound) cleaned small black mussels
- 400g (12½ ounces) skinless white fish fillets, cut into 4cm (1½-inch) pieces
- 1 cup (120g) frozen peas
- ⅓ cup coarsely chopped fresh flat-leaf parsley

aïoli

- 1 cup (300g) mayonnaise
- 2 tablespoons lemon juice
- 2 cloves garlic, crushed

1 Combine saffron and the boiling water in a small heatproof bowl.

2 Heat oil in a 40cm (16-inch) round shallow frying pan; cook onion over medium heat, stirring, about 10 minutes or until soft and golden brown. Add garlic; cook, stirring, 1 minute. Add tomato; cook, stirring frequently, about 15 minutes or until pulpy.

3 Meanwhile, shell and devein prawns, leaving tails intact.

4 Stir saffron mixture, paprika, the water and rice into pan; bring to the boil. Reduce heat, place mussels, prawns and fish on top of rice (do not stir to combine); simmer, uncovered, without stirring, about 20 minutes or until rice is almost tender. Sprinkle peas into pan; simmer, uncovered, about 3 minutes or until liquid is absorbed. Remove pan from heat, cover; stand 10 minutes. Season to taste; stir in parsley.

5 Meanwhile, make aïoli. Serve paella with aïoli.

aïoli Combine ingredients in small serving bowl.

serves 6
nutritional count per serving 28.2g total fat (4g saturated fat); 2897kJ (693 cal); 68.9g carbohydrate; 38.2g protein; 4.3g fibre

veal cutlets with green olive salsa

- 2 tablespoons olive oil
- 2 cloves garlic, crushed
- 1 tablespoon finely chopped fresh oregano
- 2 teaspoons finely grated lemon rind
- 1 tablespoon lemon juice
- 4 x 125g (4 ounce) veal cutlets

green olive salsa

- 1 tablespoon lemon juice
- ¼ cup coarsely chopped fresh flat-leaf parsley
- ½ cup (80g) finely chopped large green olives
- 1 small green capsicum (bell pepper) (150g), chopped finely
- 1 tablespoon olive oil
- 1 clove garlic, crushed
- 1 tablespoon finely chopped fresh oregano

1 Make green olive salsa.

2 Combine oil, garlic, oregano, rind and juice in a small bowl; brush mixture over veal. Cook veal on a heated oiled grill plate (or grill or barbecue) until browned both sides and cooked as desired.

3 Serve veal with salsa.

green olive salsa

Combine ingredients in a small bowl.

serving suggestion

Serve with barbecued kipfler potatoes (see tip).

tip To make barbecued kipflers, boil, steam or microwave 1.5kg (3 pounds) kipfler potatoes until tender; drain. Halve lengthways. Combine ¼ cup fresh thyme leaves, 1 tablespoon coarsely grated lemon rind, 2 crushed garlic cloves, ⅓ cup olive oil, ¼ cup lemon juice and potato in large bowl. Cook potato on a heated oiled grill plate (or grill or barbecue) about 15 minutes or until browned.

serves 4
nutritional count per serving 16.3g total fat (2.7g saturated fat); 1112kJ (266 cal); 5.8g carbohydrate; 23.4g protein; 1.2g fibre

dessert

Famed for siestas and sangria, luscious desserts may be Spain's best kept secret. The Spanish offer a unique take on many of our most-loved desserts, so they're perfect for entertaining.

tips We used a sauternes-style dessert wine for this recipe. We used a 5cm (2-inch) fluted round cutter. You could also use a 5cm (2-inch) fluted square cutter or a fluted pastry cutter wheel to cut squares from pastry.

honey-wine pastries

- **2 cups (300g) plain (all-purpose) flour**
- **½ teaspoon ground cinnamon**
- **½ teaspoon finely grated lemon rind**
- **⅓ cup (80ml) light olive oil**
- **⅔ cup (160ml) sweet dessert wine**
- **vegetable oil, for deep-frying**
- **1 tablespoon icing (confectioners') sugar**
- **½ cup (180g) honey**
- **½ teaspoon whole cloves**
- **1 cinnamon stick**
- **2 star anise**

1 Sift flour and ground cinnamon into a medium bowl; stir in rind, oil and wine to form a soft dough. Knead dough on a floured surface until smooth. Cover with plastic wrap; stand 30 minutes.

2 Divide pastry in half; roll each piece between sheets of baking paper until 5mm (¼ inch) thick. Cut 5cm (2-inch) fluted rounds from pastry; gather any scraps together and re-roll, resting the pastry again for around 10 minutes before you do so.

3 Heat oil in a large saucepan; deep-fry pastries, in batches, until browned lightly. Drain on absorbent paper; dust with sifted icing sugar.

4 Meanwhile, bring honey, cloves, cinnamon stick and star anise to the boil in a small saucepan. Boil, uncovered, 2 minutes. Strain syrup into a small heatproof jug; discard spices. Cool 5 minutes.

5 Transfer pastries to a plate, drizzle with syrup.

makes 36
nutritional count per pastry 2.1g total fat (0.3g saturated fat); 297kJ (71 cal); 11g carbohydrate; 0.9g protein; 0.3g fibre

PREP & COOK TIME
35
MINUTES
(+ STANDING)

- 3 eggs
- 1 cup (220g) caster (superfine) sugar
- 1 tablespoon finely grated orange rind
- 2¼ cups (335g) self-raising flour
- ¼ cup (60ml) orange juice
- ½ cup (125ml) skim milk
- 1 cup (250ml) extra virgin olive oil
- ½ cup (125ml) orange juice, warmed, extra
- ¼ cup (40g) icing (confectioners') sugar

1 Preheat oven to 200°C/400°F. Oil a deep 22cm (9-inch) square cake pan.

2 Beat eggs, caster sugar and rind in a medium bowl with an electric mixer until thick and creamy and sugar is dissolved. Stir in sifted flour, then combined juice, milk and oil, in three batches. Pour mixture into pan.

3 Bake cake about 45 minutes. Stand cake in pan 5 minutes; turn, top-side up, onto a wire rack placed over a tray.

4 Pour extra juice over hot cake; dust with sifted icing sugar. Cool cake before serving.

olive oil cake

PREP & COOK TIME 1 HOUR 10 MINS (+ COOLING)

serves 10
nutritional count per serving 24.8g total fat (3.8g saturated fat); 1526kJ (365 cal); 51.8g carbohydrate; 5.9g protein; 1.3g fibre

serves 8
nutritional count per serving 7g total fat (4.2g saturated fat); 903kJ (216 cal); 52.2g carbohydrate; 5.6g protein; 0g fibre

crema catalana

- **8 egg yolks**
- **1 cup (220g) caster (superfine) sugar**
- **1.125 litres (4½ cups) milk**
- **2 teaspoons finely grated lemon rind**
- **1 cinnamon stick**
- **½ cup (75g) cornflour (cornstarch)**
- **⅓ cup (75g) caster (superfine) sugar, extra**

1 Whisk egg yolks and sugar in a large bowl until creamy.
2 Stir 1 litre (4 cups) of the milk, rind and cinnamon in a large saucepan over medium heat until mixture just comes to the boil. Remove immediately from heat.
3 Strain milk into a large heatproof jug; gradually whisk milk mixture into egg mixture. Blend cornflour with remaining milk in a small jug; whisk into egg mixture.
4 Return mixture to pan; cook, stirring, until mixture boils and thickens.
5 Pour mixture into a 26cm (10½-inch) heatproof pie dish; cover, refrigerate 4 hours or overnight.
6 Just before serving, sprinkle with extra sugar; cook under a preheated grill (broiler) until sugar is caramelised.

PREP & COOK TIME
30
MINUTES

churros

- **1 cup (250ml) water**
- **1 tablespoon caster (superfine) sugar**
- **90g (3 ounces) butter, chopped coarsely**
- **1 cup (150g) plain (all-purpose) flour**
- **2 eggs**
- **vegetable oil, for deep-frying**

aniseed sugar

- **5 star anise**
- **½ cup (110g) caster (superfine) sugar**

1 Make aniseed sugar.

2 Bring the water, sugar and butter to the boil in a medium saucepan. Add sifted flour; beat with a wooden spoon over high heat until mixture comes away from base and sides of pan to form a smooth ball. Transfer mixture to small bowl; beat in eggs, one at a time, with electric mixer until mixture becomes glossy.

3 Spoon mixture into a piping bag fitted with a 1cm (½-inch) fluted tube.

4 Heat oil in a large saucepan; pipe 6cm (2¼-inch) lengths of batter into oil (cut off lengths with a knife). Deep-fry churros, in batches, about 6 minutes or until browned lightly and crisp. Drain on absorbent paper.

5 Roll churros in aniseed sugar. Serve warm.

aniseed sugar Blend or process ingredients until ground finely.

makes 35
nutritional count per churros 3.4g total fat (1.6g saturated fat); 247kJ (59 cal); 6.8g carbohydrate; 0.9g protein; 0.2g fibre

ALMONDS flat, pointy-tipped nut with a pitted brown shell; its creamy white kernel is covered by a brown skin.
slivered small pieces cut lengthways.
BAY LEAVES aromatic leaves from the bay tree available fresh or dried; adds a strong, slightly peppery flavour.
BEANS
green also called french or string beans, this long thin fresh bean is consumed in its entirety once cooked.
white a generic term we use for canned or dried cannellini, haricot, navy or great northern beans.
BEEF, SKIRT lean, flavourful coarse-grained cut from the inner thigh. Needs slow-cooking; good for stews or casseroles.
BEETROOT (BEETS) firm, round root vegetable.
BICARBONATE OF SODA also called baking soda.
BREADCRUMBS
packaged prepared fine-textured but crunchy white breadcrumbs; good for coating foods that are to be fried.
stale crumbs made by grating, blending or processing 1- or 2-day-old bread.
BUTTER we use salted butter unless stated.
CAPERS grey-green buds of a warm climate shrub, sold dried and salted or pickled in a vinegar brine; young ones (baby capers) are available in brine or dried in salt.

CAPSICUM (BELL PEPPER) belong to the same family as hot chillies, but do not contain heat. Known as pimiento in Spain. Capsicums are green when unripe, and ripen to red, yellow, purple-black or brown.
CAYENNE PEPPER a thin-fleshed, long, very hot dried red chilli, usually available ground.
CHEESE
manchego a famous semi-firm Spanish sheep's cheese which is mild when young, but after ageing for 3 months or longer, becomes a rich golden colour and develops a full, tangy flavour with the characteristic aftertaste of sheep's milk.
parmesan also called parmigiano; a hard, grainy cow's-milk cheese originating in the Parma region of Italy. The curd is salted in brine for a month then aged for up to 2 years.
CHICKEN
breast fillet breast halved, skinned, boned.
small chicken also called spatchcock or poussin; no more than 6 weeks old, weighing a maximum of 500g.
tenderloins thin strip of meat lying just under the breast.
thigh cutlets thigh with skin and centre bone intact; sometimes found skinned with bone intact.
thigh fillets thigh with skin and centre bone removed.

CHICKPEAS (GARBANZO BEANS) an irregularly round, sandy-coloured legume. Available canned or dried (soak several hours in water before use).
CHILLI use rubber gloves when handling fresh chillies as they can burn your skin. We use unseeded chillies as the seeds contain the heat.
ancho mild, dried chillies commonly used in Mexican cooking.
flakes also sold as crushed chilli; dehydrated deep-red extremely fine slices and whole seeds.
green any unripened chilli; also particular varieties that are ripe when green, such as jalapeño, habanero, poblano or serrano.
jalapeño pronounced *hah-lah-pain-yo*. Fairly hot, medium-sized, plump, dark green chilli; available pickled, sold canned or bottled, and fresh, from greengrocers.
CHOCOLATE, DARK EATING (SEMI-SWEET) contains a high percentage of cocoa liquor and cocoa butter, and little added sugar. It is ideal for use in desserts and cakes.
CHORIZO small, coarse-textured pork and beef sausages. Deeply smoked, very spicy and dry-cured so they do not need cooking. Can be purchased fresh.
CINNAMON available in pieces (sticks or quills) and ground into powder.

glossary

CLOVES dried flower buds of a tropical tree; used whole or ground. Have a strong scent and taste so use sparingly.

COCOA POWDER also known as unsweetened cocoa.

CORNFLOUR also called cornstarch.

CREAM

pouring also known as pure cream. It has no additives, and contains a minimum fat content of 35 per cent.

thickened a whipping cream that contains a thickener (minimum fat content of 35 per cent).

CUCUMBER, LEBANESE also known as european or burpless cucumber; short, slender and thin-skinned.

CUMIN also called zeera or comino; resembling caraway in size, cumin is the dried seed of a parsley-related plant with a spicy, almost curry-like flavour. Available dried as seeds or ground.

DILL also called dill weed; used fresh or dried, in seed form or ground. Its feathery, frond-like fresh leaves are grassier and more subtle than the dried version or the seeds.

EGGPLANT also called aubergine. Ranging in size from tiny to very large and in colour from pale green to deep purple. Can also be purchased char-grilled, packed in oil, in jars.

EGGS we use large (60g) chicken eggs. If a recipe calls for raw or barely cooked eggs, exercise caution if there is a salmonella problem in your area, particularly in food eaten by children and pregnant women.

FLOUR

plain unbleached wheat flour is the best for baking: the gluten content ensures a strong dough, which produces a light result.

rice very fine, almost powdery, gluten-free flour; made from ground white rice.

self-raising plain or wholemeal flour with baking powder and salt added; make at home in the proportion of 1 cup flour to 2 teaspoons baking powder.

KUMARA the Polynesian name of an orange-fleshed sweet potato often confused with yam; good baked, boiled, mashed or fried similarly to other potatoes.

LENTILS (red, brown, yellow) dried pulses often identified by and named after their colour. Eaten by cultures all over the world, most famously perhaps in the dhals of India, lentils have high food value.

MAYONNAISE we use whole-egg mayonnaise; a commercial product of high quality made with whole eggs and labelled as such.

MILK we use full-cream homogenised milk unless stated otherwise.

NUTMEG a strong and pungent spice ground from the dried nut of a native Indonesian tree. Grate your own for a stonger flavour.

OIL

olive made from ripened olives. Extra virgin and virgin are the first and second press, respectively, and are therefore considered the best; the "extra light" or "light" on other types refers to taste not fat levels.

vegetable any number of oils from plant rather than animal fats.

OLIVES olives are eaten green (unripe) and black (ripe). Both are inedibly bitter when picked and must be leached of their bitter juices by salt-curing or brining. Green olives are firm and tangy; available pitted, stone-in or stuffed. Black olives are more mellow in flavour than green ones and are softer in texture; available stone-in, pitted and sliced.

OREGANO also called wild marjoram; has a woody stalk and clumps of tiny, dark-green leaves. Has a pungent, peppery flavour.

PAPRIKA ground dried, sweet red capsicum (bell pepper); varieties available include sweet, hot, mild and smoked.

POLENTA also known as cornmeal; a flour-like cereal made of dried corn (maize). Also the dish made from it.

POTATO

baby new also called chats; not a separate variety but an early harvest with very thin skin. Good unpeeled steamed, eaten hot or cold in salads.

bintje oval, creamy skin, yellow flesh; good all-purpose potato, great baked and fried, good in salads.

kipfler small, finger-shaped, nutty flavour; great baked and in salads.

russet burbank long and oval, rough white skin with shallow eyes, white flesh; good for baking and frying.

QUAIL related to the pheasant and partridge; a small, delicate-flavoured farmed game bird ranging in weight from 250g to 300g.

RICE

calasparra Spanish short-grain rice absorbs three times its own volume of liquid, while keeping its firm shape; perfectly suited to making paella.

long-grain elongated grains that remain separate when cooked; this is the most popular steaming rice in Asia.

short-grain fat, almost round grain with a high starch content; tends to clump together when cooked.

SAFFRON the stigma (three per flower) of the saffron crocus. Imparts a yellow-orange colour to food once infused – use with restraint as too much can overwhelm other flavours. Quality can vary greatly and the best is the most expensive spice in the world. Nearly three-quarters of the world's saffron comes from Spain.

SEAFOOD

anchovies fillets are preserved and packed in oil or salt in small cans or jars, and are strong in flavour. Fresh anchovies are much milder in flavour.

mussels should only be bought from a reliable fish market: they must be tightly closed when bought, indicating they are alive. Before cooking, scrub shells with a strong brush to remove beards; do not eat any that do not open after cooking.

prawns (shrimp) can be bought uncooked (green) or cooked, with or without shells.

sardines small oily fish. Sardines are commonly purchased canned (tightly packed in oil or brine); fresh sardines are also available and grilled, pickled or smoked.

scallops a type of bivalve; often eaten raw or barely seared, they should never be cooked more than 30 seconds as they will lose their juicy tenderness and be tough.

squid also known as calamari; a type of mollusc. Buy squid hoods to make preparation and cooking faster.

white fish non-oily fish; includes bream, flathead, whiting, snapper, redfish, dhufish, ling.

SHERRY a fortified wine made from white grapes grown near Jerez, Spain.

STAR ANISE a dried star-shaped pod. seeds have an astringent aniseed flavour.

SUGAR

brown a soft, finely granulated sugar retaining molasses for colour and flavour.

caster also called superfine or finely granulated table sugar.

icing also known as confectioners' sugar or powdered sugar; pulverised granulated sugar crushed together with a small amount of cornflour.

pure icing also known as confectioners' sugar or powdered sugar.

TOMATO

canned whole peeled tomatoes in natural juices; available crushed, chopped or diced. Use undrained.

egg (plum) also called roma; small, oval-shaped tomatoes.

TURMERIC also called kamin; is a rhizome related to galangal and ginger. Fresh turmeric can be substituted with the more commonly found dried powder.

VANILLA

bean dried, long, thin pod; the minuscule black seeds inside are used to impart a vanilla flavour.

extract obtained from vanilla beans infused in water; a non-alcoholic version of essence.

WITLOF also called belgian endive; related to and confused with chicory.

ZUCCHINI also called courgette; harvested when young, its edible flowers can be stuffed and deep-fried.

conversion chart

measures

One Australian metric measuring cup holds approximately 250ml, one Australian metric tablespoon holds 20ml, one Australian metric teaspoon holds 5ml. The difference between one country's measuring cups and another's is within a 2- or 3-teaspoon variance, and will not affect your cooking results. North America, New Zealand and the United Kingdom use a 15ml tablespoon. All cup and spoon measurements are level. The most accurate way of measuring dry ingredients is to weigh them. When measuring liquids, use a clear glass or plastic jug with metric markings. We use large eggs with an average weight of 60g.

dry measures

METRIC	IMPERIAL
15g	½oz
30g	1oz
60g	2oz
90g	3oz
125g	4oz (¼lb)
155g	5oz
185g	6oz
220g	7oz
250g	8oz (½lb)
280g	9oz
315g	10oz
345g	11oz
375g	12oz (¾lb)
410g	13oz
440g	14oz
470g	15oz
500g	16oz (1lb)
750g	24oz (1½lb)
1kg	32oz (2lb)

liquid measures

METRIC	IMPERIAL
30ml	1 fluid oz
60ml	2 fluid oz
100ml	3 fluid oz
125ml	4 fluid oz
150ml	5 fluid oz
190ml	6 fluid oz
250ml	8 fluid oz
300ml	10 fluid oz
500ml	16 fluid oz
600ml	20 fluid oz
1000ml (1 litre)	1¾ pints

length measures

METRIC	IMPERIAL
3mm	⅛in
6mm	¼in
1cm	½in
2cm	¾in
2.5cm	1in
5cm	2in
6cm	2½in
8cm	3in
10cm	4in
13cm	5in
15cm	6in
18cm	7in
20cm	8in
23cm	9in
25cm	10in
28cm	11in
30cm	12in (1ft)

oven temperatures

These oven temperatures are only a guide for conventional ovens. For fan-forced ovens, check the manufacturer's manual.

	°C (CELSIUS)	°F (FAHRENHEIT)
Very slow	120	250
Slow	150	275-300
Moderately slow	160	325
Moderate	180	350-375
Moderately hot	200	400
Hot	220	425-450
Very hot	240	475

The imperial measurements used in these recipes are approximate only. Measurements for cake pans are approximate only. Using same-shaped cake pans of a similar size should not affect the outcome of your baking. We measure the inside top of the cake pan to determine sizes.

A

aïoli 63
  green onion 20
anchovies
  cauliflower with garlic, chilli
    and anchovies 37

B

beef
  shredded beef soup 46
braised chicken with chickpeas,
  lemon & garlic 60

C

cake, olive oil 70
caper dressing 39
cauliflower with garlic, chilli
  and anchovies 37
chicken
  braised with chickpeas,
    lemon & garlic 60
  chocolate sauce, with 59
  lemon chilli chicken and
    chorizo skewers 10
  lentil salad, with 42
chickpeas
  braised chicken with
    chickpeas, lemon & garlic 60
chilli
  cauliflower with garlic, chilli
    and anchovies 37
chorizo
  chorizo and
    potato fritters 15
  fried with garlic 28
  lemon chilli chicken and
    chorizo skewers 10
churros 73
clams with white wine
  and tomatoes 40
cod
  olive fritters, and 9
  salted with roasted
    tomatoes 54
crabs
  soft shell crabs with green
    onion aïoli 20
crema catalana 71
crispy marinated whitebait 17
croquettes, paella 31
crumbed sardines with roasted
  tomato sauce 32

D

dessert
  churros 73
  crema catalana 71
  honey-wine pastries 68
  olive oil cake 70
dinner
  braised chicken with
    chickpeas, lemon & garlic 60
  chicken with chocolate
    sauce 59
  fish with green sauce
    and white bean puree 57
  salted cod with
    roasted tomatoes 54
  seafood paella with aioli 63
  veal cutlets with green
    olive salsa 64
dips
  sardine 16
dressing
  caper 39
  mint 45

E

eggplant fritters 24

F

fish see seafood
fried chorizo with
  garlic 28
fried oysters with salsa 18
fritters
  chorizo and potato 15
  cod and olive 9
  eggplant 24

G

garlic
  braised chicken with
    chickpeas, lemon & garlic 60
  cauliflower with garlic, chilli
    and anchovies 37
  fried chorizo with garlic 28
  prawns 36
green olive salsa 64
green onion aïoli 20

H

honey-wine pastries 68

L

lemon
  braised chicken with
    chickpeas, lemon & garlic 60
  chilli chicken and chorizo
    skewers 10
lunch
  cauliflower with garlic, chilli
    and anchovies 37
  chicken with lentil salad 42
  clams with white wine
    and tomatoes 40
  garlic prawns 36
  quail with tomatoes and
    mint dressing 45
  sardines with tomatoes
    and caper dressing 39
  shredded beef soup 46
  tortilla with tomato salsa 51
  Valencian salad 49

M

meatball, spiced with
  romesco sauce 27
mint dressing 45

O

olive
  cod and olive fritters 9
  green olive salsa 64
  olive oil cake 70
orange-glazed squid 22
oysters, fried with salsa 18

index

P

paella
  croquettes 31
  seafood paella
    with aioli 63
pastries, honey-wine 68
potatoes
  chorizo and potato fritters 15
  roasted thyme potatoes
    with spicy sauce 13
prawns
  garlic 36
  garlic herb butter, with 29

Q

quail
  tomatoes and mint
    dressing, with 45

R

roasted thyme potatoes
  with spicy sauce 13
romesco sauce 27

S

salad
  chicken with lentil 42
  Valencian 49
salsa
  fried oysters with 18
  green olive 64
salted cod with roasted
  tomatoes 54
sangria, white 6
sardine
  crumbed with roasted
    tomato sauce 32
  dip 16
  tomatoes and caper
    dressing, with 39
sauces
  green 57
  roasted tomato 32
  romesco 27
  spicy 13
seafood
  clams with white wine
    and tomatoes 40
  cod and olive fritters 9
  crispy marinated whitebait 17
  crumbed sardines with
  roasted
    tomato sauce 32
  fish with green sauce and
    white bean puree 57
  fried oysters with salsa 18
  garlic prawns 36
  orange-glazed squid 22
  prawns with garlic
    herb butter 29
  salted cod with roasted
    tomatoes 54
  sardine dip 16
  sardines with tomatoes and
    caper dressing 39
  seafood paella with aioli 63
  soft shell crabs with green
    onion aïoli 20
shredded beef soup 46
skewers
  lemon chilli chicken
    and chorizo 10
soft shell crabs with green
  onion aïoli 20
soup
  shredded beef 46
spiced meatballs with
  romesco sauce 27
spicy sauce 13
squid, orange-glazed 22

T

tapas
  chorizo and potato fritters 15
  cod and olive fritters 9
  crispy marinated whitebait 17
  crumbed sardines with
    roasted tomato sauce 32
  eggplant fritters 24
  fried chorizo with garlic 28
  fried oysters with salsa 18
  lemon chilli chicken and
    chorizo skewers 10
  orange-glazed squid 22
  paella croquettes 31
  prawns with garlic
    herb butter 29
  roasted thyme potatoes with
    spicy sauce 13
  sardine dip 16
  soft shell crabs with green
    onion aïoli 20
  spiced meatballs with
    romesco sauce 27
  white sangria 6
thyme
  roasted thyme potatoes
    with spicy sauce 13
tomato
  roasted tomato sauce 32
  salsa 51
  salted cod
    with roasted tomatoes 54
tortilla with tomato salsa 51

V

Valencian salad 49
veal cutlets with green
  olive salsa 64

W

white sangria 6
whitebait, crispy marinated 17

Published in 2013 by Bauer Media Books, Sydney
Bauer Media Books are published by Bauer Media Limited
54 Park St, Sydney
GPO Box 4088, Sydney, NSW 2001.
phone (02) 9282 8618; fax (02) 9126 3702
www.awwcookbooks.com.au

BAUER MEDIA BOOKS
Publisher – Sally Wright
Editorial & Food Director – Pamela Clark
Creative Director – Hieu Chi Nguyen
Food Concept Director – Sophia Young
Director of Sales, Marketing & Rights – Brian Cearnes

Published and Distributed in the United Kingdom by Octopus Publishing Group
Endeavour House
189 Shaftesbury Avenue
London WC2H 8JY
United Kingdom
phone (+44)(0)207 632 5400; fax (+44)(0)207 632 5405
info@octopus-publishing.co.uk;
www.octopusbooks.co.uk

To order books:
telephone LBS on 01903 828 503
order online at
www.australian-womens-weekly.com
or www.octopusbooks.co.uk

Printed in Thailand
International foreign language rights, Brian Cearnes, Bauer Media Books
bcearnes@bauer-media.com.au

A catalogue record for this book is available from the British Library.
ISBN 978-1-90742-869-2

ABN 18 053 273 546

First published in 2013. Reprinted 2013.